My parents Robert and Delores Bozeman, for teaching me how to sacrifice for others.

My Pastor, Corey B. Brooks, for his radical faith, Godly leadership, and trusting me to extend the vision to Atlanta as a church planter.

The entire New Beginnings Church of Chicago/Atlanta families.

My beautiful wife Sheila, God's gift to me, for always being there for me and our children, highs and lows, when we had it and when we didn't, being patient and understanding during my time of ministering to others and walking with me on this faith journey every step of the way.

CONTENTS

God Takes No Pleasure In Making Life Hard

Friends, when life gets really difficult, don't jump to the conclusion that God isn't on the job. Instead, be glad that you are in the very thick of what Christ experienced. This is a spiritual refining process, with glory just around the corner. — **1 Peter 4:12-13 (MSG)**

For he does not enjoy hurting people or causing them sorrow. — **Lamentations 3:33 (NLT)**

Your problems have purpose. But, needless to say, we all have problems. And all of us can identify with problems on one level or another, be it directly or indirectly.

They belong to your friend, they belong to your husband, they belong to your wife, they belong to your boyfriend, they belong to your girlfriend, they belong to your children, your coworkers, your classmates, your boss … no one is exempt!

But what I want you to learn about the whole aspect of having problems is that they have *purpose*. Yes, that's right, a meaningful intent, non-accidental but orchestrated, controlled chaos that doesn't feel good on any day or any level, and I'm supposed to understand this—got it!

The only thing that matters is that God alone can fix your problem.

I know, I know. The problem still may not be *yours*. But it could be yours tomorrow.

Let me ask you something. Have you ever heard those dreaded words come out of the mouth of the clerk behind the counter or the representative on the phone: "I'm sorry, *but...*"?

Typically, when you're faced with a problem, you simply want the person you're expressing your problem to—to just fix it. To answer the question. Offer the solution. Reverse the charge. Give the refund.

Now, those kinds of problems are somewhat simplistic. But what about those deeper problems? The ones that affect your emotional and spiritual levels. The ones that make you question your value and your worth. The ones that make you question why you were even born. There's got to be more to life than this!

You might have to deal with problems that were never yours to begin with. Maybe they originated in your mother's womb. Or stemmed from your father's past. Your problems might be the outcome of someone else's wrongdoings.

It doesn't matter how the problem came to you. It doesn't matter if it came from your father, your mother, your grandparents, or someone who claimed to be your friend. It doesn't matter if it's a generational curse or an ungodly soul tie. It doesn't matter if it's ignorance, another person with a really bad attitude, a demon, or Satan himself.

The only thing that matters is that God alone can fix your problem.

Don't take a problem personally. If you do, you will miss the purpose behind the problem.

Here's the thing, though: When you don't understand the purpose of your problem, you are subject to make your problem bigger than it was ever intended to be.

It is crucial to understand that the problem God has given you has mighty purpose. Embracing this truth will prevent you from going crazy or taking the problem personally.

Don't take a problem personally. If you do, you will miss the purpose behind the problem.

God uses your problems for on-the-job training. He makes your problem your teacher. But when you fail to recognize your problem as your teacher, all sorts of struggles arise. If you don't see your problem as a teacher, it will become your torturer!

Your doubt, disbelief, and ignorance can turn a normal, natural problem into an abnormal, supernatural problem, all because you didn't see the purpose behind the problem.

If God is all-knowing and all-powerful, why does He allow problems to come into our lives?

God is God. He is sovereign. He can remove the problem if He wants to. Knowing this, you might cry out, "God, why did you allow this awful thing to happen to me? Why did you allow me to go through what I went through? Why didn't you make it stop? I know you could've if you wanted to."

God will never fix a problem prematurely, even if it hurts you.

Before you beg God to take away your problem, ask yourself what He's trying to teach you. God allows problems so you can have the opportunity to trust him. God will never fix a problem prematurely, even if it hurts you.

I don't care how much you have prayed, I don't care how many tongues you speak in, I don't care how many olives you have crushed to extract the oil, I don't care how many trips you've taken to Israel, I don't care how long you lay on the floor prostrate, and I don't care how many demons you have cast out. God is never going to fix a problem prematurely—even if it hurts you.

Why? Because if God had fixed your problem prematurely, the purpose He had for your life would be erased. So, why do you have to endure this problem in your life? Great question and I'm glad you asked … that's what we're going to get into next: How God uses problems in your life!

CHAPTER ONE

How God Uses Problems In Your Life

*Friends when life gets really difficult, don't jump to the
conclusion that God isn't on the job. Instead be glad that
you are in the very thick of what Christ experienced. This is
a spiritual refining process with glory just around the corner.* — **1 Peter 4:12 (MSG)**

OVER HERE!!!!

The best way to get your attention and realign your
focus, is to come face to face with a problem! The right
problem has the power to shake the very foundation of
your life as if an earthquake were happening in the mid-
dle of the night, ultimately causing you to wake up out of
a walking coma! God uses things that we least expect to
bless us—problems. Problems can either be your best
friend or your worse enemy, but that all depends on your
perspective.

God uses problems on purpose and for a purpose! We
may not like it, and may wish there was another way, but
in order to get you on the right path towards your desti-

ny, God uses problems to point us in the right direction, particularly after we've been blinded by a bad decision, stifled by a lackadaisical mindset or surprisingly, faithful in our commitment to serve others out of our love for him.

I hear you ... I can see the other two, but why would God do this to the faithful servant? Before you ask this question, you might want to consider Jesus' problem on the cross. He was faithful, he was obedient, he was sinless, but yet had to endure the negative effects of a major problem to bring about the perfect will of his Father.

God will creatively use problems in your life right under your nose. The challenge we have is that we are too close to recognize God in our situation.

Have you ever been in a relationship where God allowed you to encounter a problem just so he could release you from that relationship? Yeah, you cried. Yeah, you were hurt from the breakup, got angry at the world and all of this was a very real problem to you. But once you got out of the relationship, you saw that God created the problem to redirect your heart.

Your problem had a purpose.

One can't help but wish life were as easy as reading the Word, applying the Word and then living happily ever after, but it's not! Sometimes problems arise just so you'll turn and look at God. When you refuse to listen, problems can be the best tutors.

If you don't learn something on your own by living a life of obedience to

God, He sends a problem to be your tutor.

Everyone wants to receive blessings and gifts from God, but few want to go through the process to get the prize.

God wants to teach you lessons through the reading of His Word. But most of us don't show that kind of faithful discipline. When you don't study, that means you live your life on your own. You open the door to shame in your life. You bring all kinds of problems into your life that God never intended for you to have.

If you studied God's Word and lived the way He intended for you to live, you would never have to experience certain problems that are placed in your life to call you back to Him. But because we often refuse to do right by God, He sends us a problem that usually causes us to look to Him for help.

If you don't learn something on your own by living a life of obedience to God, He sends a problem to be your tutor.

And watch this: When you refuse to learn the lesson, God keeps that problem going on and on and on and it won't go away until you submit to the lesson.

Respect Your Problems

You might be wondering why you should respect your problems, especially after all the trouble they have caused. They don't seem worthy of much respect. Here's why they are: Everything in your life has to be allowed by God. Even the devil cannot have access to you unless

He gets permission. In Luke 22:31, Jesus says, "Simon, the enemy Satan, has asked to sift you like wheat." Satan asked because he needed permission. Your problems are not accidents. Each one has a mighty purpose. You just need to cry out to God and ask him to show you the purpose through the pain of this problem.

Many of us continually give the devil the permission slip because we refuse to learn what God wants us to learn and therefore, problems come into our lives to teach us what we refused to learn on our own.

You may recognize some of the ways we refuse:

- Refusal to submit to our spiritual fathers, mothers, and wise mentors.

- Refusal to learn from those who've had similar struggles.

- Refusal to read and study the Word, which is God's way of guiding and directing our lives.

- Refusal to have a humble, moldable heart through our problems.

God Uses Problems To Test Your Faith

Dear brothers and sisters, when troubles come your way, consider it an opportunity for great joy. For you know that when your faith is tested, your endurance has a chance to grow. — James 1:2-3

God doesn't just use problems to get our attention and realign our focus. He also uses problems to put our faith to the test. Before a car or any other product is sent to the dealership to be sold, right after it comes off the assembly line, it's put to the test. The manufacturer has to make sure it meets the advertised standards promised to entice a potential buyer. Well, God is the same way. When you come off the assembly line of salvation through the Lord Jesus Christ, He puts you to the test, to make sure you meet the advertised standards promised in His Word! Your passing this test will influence potential buyers—The Lost! When God tests you like this, it's His way of saying, "I want to see what you're made of. I want you to learn something about you that you didn't know. I want you to discover your purpose!"

Typically, if asked, people will say they have faith, but when it comes time to put it to work, their faith is nowhere to be found, replaced by fear. You never really know if you have an active faith until it's time to use it. And all a person needs to flesh out their faith, if it's there, is a Problem! Is your faith active faith or fantasy faith, meaning it's all in your mind?

Ask yourself, how much pain do you need to go through before you realize you're going in the wrong direction? How much pain do you need to suffer before you finally get it in your mind to say, "You know what? I need to change my ways because this isn't working." Problems will test you until you change... *Sometimes it takes a painful experience to make us change our ways (Proverbs 20:30, GNT).* I'm afraid some believers have become so accustomed to their problems that when they do finally come into a place of peace—peace from God—it actually becomes uncomfortable to them. They can't handle peace and quiet. They become dependent upon noise and chaos in their lives; they're not comfortable. This isn't how it should be. You should be comfortable with the peace God brings you.

What's Your Purpose In This Problem?

When problems show up, you need to speak up and ask God, *"What's my purpose in this problem?"* It doesn't matter what type of problem it is: spiritual, financial, relational, moral, etc. Ask Him "What's my purpose in this problem?" It's very dangerous to be in the dark about your existence and why you were created. Failure to know your purpose in the problem you're currently challenged with will cause mismanagement and misdirection of your life... You'll constantly find yourself in places you shouldn't be, with people you shouldn't be with, doing things you shouldn't be doing! It's not until you know your purpose that you know when to go, where to go and who to go with; you just might have to go by yourself... all of this, has nothing to do with how you feel about the matter, but what God said about the matter. In other words, never let your feelings dictate your faith but let your faith dictate your feelings!

Don't treat purpose like a visit to the doctor's office after an examination you had a week earlier and now you've been called in to get the results. However, because you think it's bad news, you're worried and scared of what the doctor might say and really don't want to hear it.

Whatever your purpose is, you want to know it so you can understand it, so while you're facing your problems, you can focus on the light at the end of the tunnel and not get derailed along the way trying to figure out your next step! Purpose has already ordered your next step... your job is to keep it movin', don't stop for anything. Get on that path as quickly as possible, learn the lesson, and store the lesson up for a rainy day; because at the end of the day, that problem is not exclusively for you. God wants this problem to make you stronger for the benefit of someone else whom you have yet to meet. They're headed down a dead end street called Bad Life Blvd. waiting on you to point them in the right direction by sharing your testimony of truth supported by godly wisdom, which you've acquired in the process of trusting God while pursuing your purpose in your problems.

Discover Who You Are In Christ

Have you ever allowed what others said about you cause you to question or doubt who you are? Sometimes God sends problems to show you that you're stronger and tougher than any lie you've been living out of ignorance or negligence to your God-ordained purpose. He shows you that there's more to you than the outside cover. There are pages and pages that you haven't even read of your own book.

And until you read the whole book of who you are in Christ—and what you can do through Him—you'll never enjoy the fulfillment of the answered call on your life. Not knowing who you are in Christ causes problems and threatens your purpose in life! Not knowing who you are is an opportunity to become who you're not. Most of us settle for the outside cover. But God says, "When I look at you, I look at what lies beyond your exterior." He doesn't care about your athleticism, your education, or your beauty. He doesn't care about your beautiful eyes or figures, sisters. He doesn't care about your biceps and triceps, brothers. God instead probes from the inside-out. He says, "I'm going to go inside and see what you're made of."

So, what are you made of? Hide Psalm 139:13-15 in your heart...

You made all the delicate, inner parts of my body and knit me together in my mother's womb.

Thank you for making me so wonderfully complex!

Your workmanship is marvelous—how well I know it.

You watched me as I was being formed in utter seclusion, as I was woven together in the dark of the womb.

You saw me before I was born.

Every day of my life was recorded in your book.

Every moment was laid out before a single day had passed. (NLT)

Look at v.14 again "How well I know it." If you didn't know, you should know now — Wonderfully Complex and Marvelous, this is you! Knowing this about yourself puts all your personal problems in their proper perspective.

Because He loves you, God has put a lot of work into you and is not about to allow a problem that you don't understand, come along and destroy all of his efforts to prepare you for a dying world that needs a witness.

God Uses Problems To Restore You

God uses problems not only to get your attention, and test your faith, but also to restore you when you're out of order. It was a problem that got you in trouble and now it's a problem that will get you out of trouble. God already knows it will be painful for you, but afterward, you'll share in His great holiness.

One of the main reasons people don't embrace God fully, is they are unwilling to take correction from Him. "God, you better not hit me, you better not touch me, you better get your hands off me," they cry.

I remember in the good old days, my mother would exercise her parental rights to discipline me or one of my siblings by way of corporal punishment - a butt whoopin' for short. There was never a time when she executed this assignment that she stopped loving us. Her goal was always to restore us or bring us back from the depraved state of being that got us in this troubled state in the first place.

So what did we do under these circumstances? We stood there and took it!

Yes, it was painful. No, you couldn't understand why someone who claims to love you could be inflicting this kind of pain on your flesh. But you took it because you knew if you didn't take the pain right then, you'd get it worse later when daddy came home and then you'd wish you were dead. This punishment was a restoration problem. If left unchecked, we would have never learned that our actions were wrong and may have begun living a reckless life. We needed to be restored back to normality.

It's the same way with God.

God uses purposeful problems to fix painful problems. You may think that your life is bad and horrible, and that nothing is going right for you. But this is just the restoration process because God loves you.

God loves you enough to restore you when you're out of order, out of balance or even out of bounds. He wants you to experience the light and holiness that Jesus is. He wants you to get close to Him. He tries to get your attention even when you keep running from Him.

But the more you run, the more it's going to hurt. Everywhere you go, there's a storm waiting. Don't believe me? Ask Jonah.

Jonah got on a boat headed for Tarshish in a state of rebellion running from God. He got on a boat, and everybody on that boat suffered from the storm that was meant to stop Jonah. That's why some of you are struggling right now.

Some of you are the *other guys* on that boat. Some of you have a problem in your life, and it's not even your problem—it belongs to the person you keep hanging out with. The person you keep bailing out. The person who constantly attracts trouble for breakfast, lunch and dinner.

God is trying to get to them, so they can be restored and you're in the way. That's why you are going through what you're going through. My suggestion for you is this: do like the men did on that boat. Throw him or her overboard and let that big fish grab 'em, and let God do what He needs to do to restore them. Get out of the way because, if you don't, it's going to cost you.

Those men had to throw all of their cargo over the side of the boat. It costs them something to try and save somebody living in a state of rebellion. So you must understand: God uses purposeful problems to punish you in an attempt to restore you on purpose.

And understand this: Punishment deals with your past bad behavior, but correction deals with your future good behavior.

Punishment deals with your past bad behavior, but correction deals with your future good behavior.

In the restoration process, some of us are going to suffer consequences because of what we've done. That's our punishment for sin. But thanks to His merciful grace, God will forgive and restore us. Yet that doesn't mean He's going to stop the consequences from coming into your life. A man robs a bank, gets caught and is found guilty, sentenced to 20 years in prison, he asks God to forgive him, God forgives and restores him, but the consequence or punishment of his sin is 20 years in prison, even though he's been restored.

And just because your consequences catch up with you doesn't mean God doesn't love you. Your consequences are punishing you from your past sin, but God is restoring you for your future and His Glory.

God Uses Problems To Stop Problems

The purpose of your problems is not only to restore you, but to protect you from problems. You may not recognize it right away, but He wants to protect you, and you need to understand that.

Now, you may be thinking: "My problem is what's hurting me. How can my problem protect me? I need protection from my problem!"

You don't need protection from your problem. It's your problem that's protecting you. *Think about it:* If God had removed that problem from your life, you might not have been here today. You might have continued to pursue that abusive relationship. You might have made that bad financial investment. You might have gotten married to the wrong person. You might have quit your job prematurely, you just might...

You don't need protection from your problem. It's your problem that's protecting you.

God puts problems in your life to protect you from others, but he also has to protect you from You! This is why He allows the present pain of a problem so you'll be protected from a future disaster you never knew was coming.

The righteous person faces many troubles, but the LORD comes to the rescue each time (Psalm 34:19, NLT).

How will He do this? By giving you another problem. Have you ever been on your way to an important engagement—you really needed to be there on time—and you ended up getting a flat tire and didn't have a spare? Grudgingly, you had to call the people you were going to meet and tell them that you couldn't make it.

So you went inside your house, turned on the television, and lo and behold, there was a multi-car accident on the same highway you were about to merge on to. You watch for a minute and then think, "Wait a minute. Had I NOT had that flat tire, I would have been in that accident and possibly in the back of that hearse at the morgue."

How about 9/11? Everybody remembers that day when the Twin Towers fell after terrorists crashed planes into them. You remember the testimonies of the people who said, "I should have been in Tower 2, except I had to drop my daughter off." Or, "I should have been in Tower 1 but overslept."

God hides purpose inside problems, so at the right moment, when needed most, you're protected, and that's why the purpose of your problem is often to protect you from something worse. But see, too many of us don't recognize God in the midst of our problems, and therefore we become self-righteous. We get caught up in our own emotions and pride and pompous attitude that we fail to give God glory even in the problem.

Thank God In The Midst Of Your Problem

When God says to give Him glory, no matter what you're going through, He means it. But so often, we get caught up in the woes of our problems that we don't honor His request.

Take a moment right now to thank God for rescuing you. Say, thank you that although I had to cancel that interview, I'm alive and didn't get in that accident. Thank you that although my heart is broken from that relationship, my heart is still beating. Thank you for my problem, Lord. Thank you Jesus!

When you learn that your problems have purpose, you'll be able to submit yourself to the leadership of the Holy Spirit. You'll be able to allow Him to navigate you through life.

Problems Will Set You Up

Purposeful problems will set you up for a successful future.

Of course, this doesn't mean you'll live a perfect life. To be "perfect" means you're going to live a life of maturity and maturity has a way of changing your perspective. What you might see as disappointments could actually be appointments God has destined for your life. In other words, we all have an appointment with disappointment – don't be late!

If you think you're going to go through life never being disappointed, you need to get out of that bubble right now because you're living in a fantasy world and need to wake up.

Everybody is going to suffer some degree of disappointment. God has it on your spiritual calendar. If you are not disappointed now, it's coming soon. So you have to understand that God uses problems to set up your future success, to mature you.

Dr. Charles Stanley says it like this: "Our heavenly Father understands our disappointment, suffering, pain, fear, and doubt. He is always there to encourage our hearts and help us understand that He's sufficient for all of our needs. When I accepted this as an absolute truth in my life, I found that my worrying stopped."

Don't Reject Your Problems

It might sound crazy, but the best thing you have going for you is your problem. Are you rejecting it or accepting it?

When you reject your problem, you're rejecting your hope of achieving your purpose in Jesus Christ.

This is why a lot of us quit. This is why a lot of us fold. This is why a lot of us can't take the slightest problem in our lives because we have no endurance and we don't trust God enough to go through the process. We quit too much...

In weight lifting, a person lifting weights will have someone called a spotter standing over them as they lift. The spotter applies just enough pressure to help you get the weight up without taking the weight off you, while at the same time encouraging you to push yourself, knowing you're in pain. The spotter knows it's resistance that builds muscle, not convenience. Well, God says, "I'm going to send you a problem on purpose and with a purpose. It's going to be your spotter."

Your purposeful problem will not take the weight of life off of you. But when you feel like the weight is going to break your neck or back or make you go crazy, your purposeful problem is going to step in and 'spot you' by lifting you up just enough while encouraging you to keep going, telling you, "You can do this"!

Let us not become weary in doing good, for at the proper time we will reap a harvest if we do not give up (Galatians 6:9).

Too many of us keep failing. Too many of us keep quitting. Too many of us keep feeling sorry for ourselves. Too many of us keep struggling with doubt and unbelief. Too many of us just won't lift our heads up and realize that what we're going through is just a training ground.

I challenge you to learn the purpose behind your problem, friend. When you do, it will grow your faith, strengthen your character, and boost your confidence in Jesus Christ. And what better place to be than in a problem that will deepen your relationship with our heavenly Father?

...I want to know Christ and experience the mighty power that raised him from the dead. I want to suffer with him, sharing in his death ... (Philippians 3:10).

Turn to God right now. Ask Him to help you see that your problems come from Heaven. Ask Him to help you break free of your personal struggles and all doubt and unbelief. Thank Him for the problems He has sent your way on purpose and with a purpose. Thank Him and pray that they will help you have a deep, personal, intimate relationship with Him, a relationship that can never be compromised, even when you have questions?

CHAPTER TWO

Why Me, God?

As Jesus was walking along, he saw a man who had been blind from birth. "Rabbi," his disciples asked him, "why was this man born blind? Was it because of his own sins or his parents' sins?"

*"It was not because of his sins or his parents' sins," Jesus answered. "This happened so the power of God could be seen in him." — **John 9:1-3 (NLT)***

If you're like me, you ask yourself these questions at some point during a problem:

Why do I have this problem? I'm trying to live right, pray consistently, walk by faith not by sight, tithe, sacrifice for others, lean not on my own understanding, follow God's direction, love my neighbor as myself, and trust in God with all of my heart.

Then you look down the hallway, up the street, around the corner and see someone who obviously does not revere the Lord and it appears as though they're prospering from a worldly standard.

Why does it seem like they are not having as many issues as I'm having—and they don't even know God?

Why, why, why?

Remember 1 Peter 4:12-13: *Dear friends, do not be surprised at the fiery ordeal that has come on you to test you, as though something strange were happening to you. But rejoice inasmuch as you participate in the sufferings of Christ, so that you may be overjoyed when his glory is revealed.*

One of the purposes of problems is to keep you in a healthy relationship with God. It's His way of drawing you to Himself. That's why God surrounds you with problems called people—be them husbands, wives, family members or friends.

A lot of us just won't seek God and pray on a consistent basis. And we need problems to lead us to Him. He loves you, He wants a relationship with you, and He recognizes that you need a good problem to make this possible.

Chances are that someone in your life has a problem that is impacting you negatively. And because of their problem, you're on your knees talking to God. Here's the point: If the problem gets you talking to God, gets you saying, "Lord, I thank you for this problem, even though it hurts. I magnify you. I exalt you," then you're in a great place.

It's much better to have problems in God's presence than to have no problems and not know where God is.

Is There Purpose In A Public Problem?

Here's something you must understand: If you don't see the problems in your life as directed by God or indirectly allowed by God, then you're going to abuse yourself. This can come in the form of low self-esteem, lack of confidence, lack of hope, zero faith, and self-hatred. And the reason you do these things is because you don't understand that you're having these problems in your life for a purpose.

Some of us are a mess. Some of us have been a mess since our birth, kind of like that blind man in John 9. We're born into problems, and that's where a lot of people are. We're born into our father's and mother's spiritual junk. Demons that are inherited, if you will. *John 9:1-2: As Jesus was walking along, he saw a man who had been blind from birth. "Rabbi," his disciples asked him, "why was this man born blind? Was it because of his own sins or his parents' sins?"*

Whereas you should have inherited your father's fortune or your mother's fortune because a good man leaves an inheritance to his children's children, instead you inherited their demons. And these demons are public—on display for others to see.

Maybe your mother was a witch, your grandmother was a witch, your great-great-grandmother was a witch, and so you've inherited witchcraft as your skill, your talent.

Or perhaps you inherited your father's low self-esteem because your grandfather was weak, and your great-grandfather was timid. Fear runs in your family all the way through the men. And now you're scared of the dark, scared of heights, scared of women, scared of men. You even jump when you see yourself in the mirror. All picked up at birth.

But what do we see when we look at John 9? Jesus' disciples asked him who had sinned because, back in that culture, whenever a child was born with a deformity, it was believed that it was a judgment by God.

When God shows off your mess, He doesn't do it just because that's what He likes to do. There's a reason, a purpose, a message in your mess.

People believed the blind man, or his parents, were being judged by God. Can you imagine having that perception on you? Can you imagine people thinking stuff about you? Some people think this way. It's a perception. "No, my kids can't play with your kids because they don't have anything in common." (Poor and rich, for instance).

Let me ask you: Have you been judged for the condition that you're in? Have you been judged for a legitimate problem you're in? Have you been judged for a problem you inherited?

But there's purpose in a public problem.

If the problem was private, you could wear a smile and fake your condition. But when your problem is in public, you can't fool anybody. This is why, sometimes, when your problem is out there for all to see, guess who allowed it to happen?

God. He's the One displaying it. And you're wondering, "Why, God?"

Here's the thing: When God shows off your mess, He doesn't do it just because that's what He likes to do. There's a reason, a purpose, a message in your mess.

There Is A Message In Your Mess

You have to understand that God is always speaking. Even when you have a messed up situation, even with a messed up marriage, even with a messed up relationship, God is always speaking.

You have God's Word, and that means God is always talking to you. You may not be able to hear the voice of God, but you'll always be able to hear the written Word. You have God's Word in your phone, on your iPad, in a hardbound book—and He's always speaking.

Even when sin separates you from God from a fellowship standpoint for a time—because if you're saved you can't break your *relationship* God, only your fellowship—He's still speaking. Because He has said, "I'll never leave you nor forsake you."

God always wants you to know what the problem is even when you are wrong. *He says if any man lacks wisdom, let him ask of God who will give liberally and won't rebuke you for that* (James 1:5). He wants you to ask:

- "Lord, what must I do to be saved?"

- "Lord, what must I do to get out of this situation?"

- "Lord, I want to repent."

God is always speaking even when you can't hear Him. In other words, there is a message in your mess even when your mess clogs your spiritual ears.

Your Problem Is A Seed For Praise

If you're trying to understand what the purpose of your problem is, recognize this: Your problem is a seed for your praise.

God oftentimes puts a problem in your life to receive praise from your mouth. Sometimes God has to plant the seed of a problem, which is all you need to start saying, "God, I thank you, I praise you, I magnify you, I exhort you, I worship you."

Remember Paul in 2 Corinthians 12:8-10, when he went to the Lord and asked Him to remove a problem from his life? And God said, "Listen, Paul, my grace is sufficient for you." See, God says when you are weak, then you are strong because His power is upon you. That's when Paul realized that he had this thing all wrong. He probably thought to himself, *I've misunderstood the problem. It has a purpose.* That's when he begins praising God for his problem. Why? Because he realizes the purpose of his problem was to make him strong.

This is a good time to just stop. Stop and thank God for whatever problem you're going through. Tell Him,

"Lord, I appreciate it. I thank you. I don't like it, but I thank you that it's making me stronger, and I give you praise."

God Does His Best Work In The Midst Of A Problem

In John 9:1-3, the man was born blind so that the Lord could do something miraculous through him. *"It was not because of his sins or his parents' sins,"* Jesus answered. *"This happened so the power of God could be seen in him"* (John 9:3).

Let me ask you something: Who would have ever thought that this blindness, this problem in his life, was put there by God so that He could display the work of the Kingdom? Think about that.

What are you going through right now? I urge you to look at Scripture again. Jesus says this man was blind so that the work of the Kingdom could be displayed in him.

Now, if that doesn't bring somebody to a place of deliverance, I don't know what will.

Picture that: God letting you go through what you're going through so that Kingdom work could be *displayed* through you.

Picture God whispering in your ear:

- *I needed the world to know that you had been abused by your alcoholic father.*

- *I needed the world to know you were a drug addict strung out, in the streets, naked.*

- *I needed the world to see you lose the house you built.*

- *I needed the world to see you lose your car through repossession.*

- *I needed the world to see you lose your wife and children to a bitter divorce.*

- *I needed the world to see you at the unemployment office.*

All so His work could be displayed through you.

It wasn't just the problem God needed people to see. He needed the world to see the problem so that they would recognize Him in the solution.

This is how God brings unbelievers to Himself. Did you know that you are a flashlight that God beams across dark places so that others would be drawn to the light of Christ in you?

I don't know about you, but when I've got a problem, I don't want anyone near me. But Jesus says: *The more you try to push people away, the more attention I will bring to your problem.*

Why? Because the number one purpose of your problem is to display the work of God through you.

Obedience Opens Blind Eyes

Can I tell you all something? Whenever you do what God has told you to do, your obedience opens your eyes to the purpose of your problem and you're able to re-solve your problem sooner rather than later.

Jesus said eight words to the blind man. *Then he spit on the ground, made mud with the saliva, and spread the mud over the blind man's eyes. He told him, "Go wash yourself in the pool of Siloam" (Siloam means "sent"). So the man went and washed and came back seeing!* (John 9:6-7). And guess what the blind man did when he heard them? He got up and did exactly what Jesus told him to do, no questions asked. Now *that* is obedience. And by his obedience, he reaped the reward of healed vision.

Imagine for a moment that you are that blind man and God just instructed you to go wash in the pool. But instead of submitting to God's instructions, you start asking questions, such as: *Why do I have to wash? Why should I put mud on my face? Did I hear you just spit on the ground?*

Until you learn to obey God, your eyes will never be opened. You'll never understand the purpose in your problem. Sure, it's natural to have questions, but God wants you to walk by faith, not by sight.

When you're faced with a problem, He wants you to:

- Praise Him in the storm.

- Step out of the boat and walk toward Him.

- Submit to Him and resist the devil.

- Trust Him with all of your heart and lean not on your own understanding.

- Acknowledge Him and allow Him to direct your path.

- Love Him with all of your heart, mind, soul, and strength—and love your neighbor as you love yourself.

Decide now to open your mouth and say, "Thank you, Jesus. Have mercy on me for feeling sorry for myself."

Take off your garment of sorrow and put on a garment of praise. It's not enough just to know the purpose of your problem. You have to walk in obedience. Because obedience opens blinded eyes.

When people asked the formerly blind man how he was able to see, he replied, "The man they call Jesus. He made some mud, put it on my eyes, and told me to go to Siloam and wash. So I went and did as he said."

Then the people brought the man to the Pharisees, some of whom were enemies of Christ. When the Pharisees found out who healed the blind man, they said, "This man (Jesus) is not from God, for he does not keep the Sabbath." But others asked how an alleged sinner could do such miraculous signs. So they were divided.

If you ever want to confuse your enemies, all you have to do is obey God.

The people who saw you blind will see you seeing. The people who saw you begging will see you loaning money to another. Because deliverance confuses your enemy.

In John 9:17, it says: "Finally, they turned again to the blind man." See how they referred to him? He's not blind anymore but they turned to the blind man because they want to operate in doubt. They are so confused that they're calling him the blind man when he's actually the man who can see.

"What have you to say about him?" the Pharisees asked. "It was your eyes that were opened."

The formerly blind man replied, "He is a prophet."

At that point they called for his parents. "Is this your son? Is this the one you say was born blind? How is it that now he can see?"

You can be kicked out of a church, but you can never be kicked out of Christ.

The parents replied: "We know he is our son, and we know he was born blind because he's our son and we've been watching over him all his life. But how he can now see or who opened up his eyes we don't know. Ask him, he is of age. He will speak for himself."

His parents said this because they were afraid. Anyone who acknowledged that Jesus was the Christ would be thrown out of the synagogue.

People who don't love Jesus want to know how you get delivered, but never want to believe.

Here's the point: If you want to understand the purpose of your problems, you must learn to speak for yourself. Learn to tell your testimony. Don't be scared of being kicked out of the synagogue. Because guess what? You can be kicked out of a church, but you can never be kicked out of Christ.

Then in John 9:24-25, the Pharisees tell the man, "Give glory to God. We know this man (Jesus) is a sinner."

And the formerly blind man replies: "Whether he's a sinner or not I don't know, but one thing I do know is I was blind but now I can see."

Then the Pharisees asked him again how he got his sight. Don't let that escape you. People who don't love Jesus want to know how you get delivered, but never want to believe.

Then the man answers the Pharisees by saying, "I've told you already and you did not listen. Why do you want to hear it again? Do you want to become one of his disciples too?"

That's when the Pharisees hurled insults at the man and said he was a disciple of Jesus.

People will accuse you of being a follower of Jesus Christ when you're delivered, and that's exactly why the Kingdom of God suffers violence.

Have you ever been talked about because God brought deliverance into your life? Have you ever been delivered by something and people start dogging you out? Deliverance is going to make you bold, and God will make a ministry out of what started as a problem.

See, there is a ministry on the other side of your obedience. Your deliverance ushers you into a ministry, just as this man who had been blind became a witness for Christ.

And when you get delivered, don't be afraid of devils. Don't be scared of people. Don't back away from Satan. Stand flat-footed in your deliverance and stand for Jesus.

In John 9:34, the Pharisees replied to the man: "You were steeped in sin at birth. How dare you lecture us!" And they threw him out.

Have you been thrown out because of your problem, or because of deliverance from your problem? Kicked out of a club, a fraternity, a sorority, a family?

Well, after Jesus heard that the Pharisees had thrown the man out, Jesus found him and said, "Do you believe in the Son of Man?"

And the man replied, "Who is he sir? Tell me so that I may believe in him."

He didn't even know he was talking to his deliverer because, when he came back from the pool, Jesus was gone. He had never seen him with his natural eyes.

So Jesus said, "You have now seen him. In fact, he is the one speaking with you."

Then the man said, "Lord, I believe." And he began to worship Christ.

After this, Jesus said that He came into the world so that the blind would see and so those who could see would become blind.

In John 9:40, some of the Pharisees heard Him say this and asked, "What, are we blind too?"

And Jesus replied, "If you were blind you would not be guilty of sin, but now that you claim you can see, your guilt remains." In other words, *you are as blind as your question.* Notice the first thing this man did when he recognized who he was looking at. He began to worship. So what is the purpose of your problem? So that you might:

- Praise him.

- Worship him.

- Stand flat-footed.

- Be bold for him.

- Bless those around you.

- Accomplish the work of Christ.

- Stand strong in the face of fear (unlike the blind man's parents who were scared).

- Be a great witness for the Lord.

- Cause people to want a relationship with Christ.

Stop sweating the small stuff. Stop getting all upset over the problem in your life. Simply do the things that God has asked of you. Obey Him, and watch as He ushers you out of blindness and into sight, by the power of His grace!

CHAPTER THREE

Find God's Grace In The Midst Of Your Problem

Out of the depths I cried to You, Lord. Lord, hear my voice.
Let your ears be attentive to my cry for mercy. If you, Lord,
kept a record of sins, who could stand? But with You there
is forgiveness so that we can with reverence serve You. —
Psalm 130:1-4

You might be on the brink of giving up because you don't understand the purpose of your problem. You might be asking, *Why Lord? Why me?* I've made it clear thus far that everything has a purpose—even problems. And that the main purpose in your problem is so the work of God can be manifest in and through you.

But now I want to challenge you to look at another passage of Scripture that describes another dimension, another level of problems, and another understanding of the purpose in problems. See, one of the biggest problems people have today is being gracious.

You would think based off of God's example in Psalm 103:1-5 that we should be willing to give and be gracious:

Let all that I am praise the LORD; with my whole heart, I will praise his holy name. Let all that I am praise the LORD; may I never forget the good things he does for me.

He forgives all my sins and heals all my diseases. He redeems me from death and crowns me with love and tender mercies. He fills my life with good things. My youth is renewed like the eagle's!

Have you done something today to be a blessing to the Lord? Or did you live this day for yourself, yourself, and yourself?

Now I want you to ask yourself, "Have I done what God has commissioned me to do today?" See, God woke you up today to fulfill His purpose and His will. Have you remotely tapped in to that today? Have you done something today to be a blessing to the Lord? Or did you live this day for yourself, yourself, and yourself?

God says, whatever you do, do it to my glory (1 Corinthians 10:31). Our tendency is to just focus on our problems. To say, "Woe is me. Why me? Woe is me." To look in the mirror of despair, despondency, and depression and ignore the blessing of being able to inhale, exhale, and recognize that we're not under the ground—but on top of it.

As believers in the Lord Jesus Christ, He purchased us, He bought us, He redeemed us, He restored us, He's our refuge, our strength, our strong tower, our shield, our Wonderful Counselor, our Everlasting Father, our Prince of Peace, Savior, Deliverer, and Healer. Need I go on? We must remember this and rejoice!

God is omnipotent, which means He is all-powerful. He is omniscient, which means He is all-knowing. He is omnipresent, which means He is everywhere at the same time, all the time.

Some run to horoscopes, witchcraft, and the occult, entertaining the methodologies of the devil without embracing the fact that our God knows everything.

See, God has The J29:11 plan for you (Jeremiah 29:11), and it's a plan for good and not evil. Have you forgotten this? Until you get to that place where your total body, soul, and spirit understand your purpose for living, your purpose for existing, your purpose for being made from nothing into something, is to bring honor and glory to God, your living is in vain!

When you forget this, you have a real problem. Because you won't be able to fulfill the promises God has laid out for you, the mandate and call upon our lives. In other words, you'll never know why you exist. That's a real problem.

God's Grace Extends To Your Problems

John Piper says this: "Grace is not simply leniency when we have sinned. Grace is the enabling gift of God not to sin. Grace is power, not just pardon."

Think about that.

The grace that God extends to us extends to us in our problems. He doesn't just give us grace for the purpose of pardoning us from our sins. He gives us grace that enables us not to sin against God.

So if we are to understand the text we are looking at, if we are going to understand the purpose of our problems, you need to understand that you will always need God's grace.

In Psalm 130:1-2, it says: "Out of the depths I cried to you, Lord. Lord hear my voice, let your ears be attentive to my cry for mercy."

You might be so deep in the depth of your circumstances and situation that it's hard for you to breathe.

You think about what you are going through, what you're struggling with, and you think about the times you've thought about killing yourself—believing in your mind that everything would be easier if you just died.

This is like this Psalm. *Lord, I cry to you, I'm reaching out to you. Father, I'm praying to you.*

Do you know what it means to be on the brink of losing your mind because of what you're dealing with, what you're going through, what your family is going through, what your children are going through? Have you ever prayed out of the depths of despair? Have you ever prayed from a place of depression? Have you ever tried to pray and the only thing you can get out is, "Lord Jesus, help me; Jesus, help me; Lord have mercy!"

So you must understand that God often allows problems in your life so that you will have a greater need for His grace and love.

You couldn't even go into the details because you felt the weight of the problem so heavy on you that it cut off your vocal cords.

Right now, this might be where you are in a problem and now you see just how much you need God's grace. But not all do this. Some try to overcome problems without the grace of God.

Grace is like life support. It pumps air in and out of your lungs. Try holding your breath for as long as you can, then start breathing again. About 5 to 10 seconds in, you wanted to take another breath, you needed to take another breath. That's because you're on life support. You need grace.

See, God will oftentimes allow us to have problems because He wants to give us grace—He wants us to experience His love at another level.

The best way for you to understand how God feels about you is to get into a problem that calls on His ability, His strength, and His might.

God's love is unconditional, which means there is nothing you can do to change how He feels about you. There's no sin you can commit that will cause God to love you less, and there is no righteous deed you can do that will cause God to love you more. His love is equal to all. You cannot earn it or gain more of it.

So you must understand that God often allows problems in your life so that you will have a greater need for His grace and love.

Many don't recognize that they have a need for God's unconditional love. They don't understand what it means to experience it, feel it, and comprehend it in their psyche. And one of the purposes of our problems is to help us better understand God's love.

Your problem might be heavier than anything you've ever felt. It might be more painful than any pain you've ever experienced. And this is the level of love that God wants you to tap into.

God does not want you to settle on what I call a one-way love relationship. He doesn't want you to be content with how you *feel* about Him. He wants you to understand how He feels about *you*. And the best way for you to understand how God feels about you is to get into a problem that calls on His ability, His strength, and His might.

God may not always be the initiator of your problem, but He is the One who can orchestrate the solution to the problem.

That's why you must recognize that you need God's grace, His love.

One problem many of us have is that we don't mind receiving God's grace, but we struggle to give God's grace to others. We don't mind getting grace when we're in sin, but when other people around us have problems we want to act like God and judge who deserves grace and who doesn't.

Let's be honest: You probably don't give out half the grace you receive.

God wants you to know that He's the One who is keeping you breathing. He wants you to know that you must live off of His grace.

God may not always be the initiator of your problem, but He is the One who can orchestrate the solution to the problem.

Oftentimes God allows problems in your life so you can learn how much He loves you. If you don't ever have a problem, you will never understand how great He is. You want to get to that place where every day you wake up and you just declare, "How great is my God." You want to make it personal. You want all the world to see how great God is. Sometimes, it's not until you get to the brink of death that you recognize how great He is.

So what about you? Do you praise God in your problems? Remember, problems teach you how to praise and declare how great God is.

Don't be the person who receives grace, but never gives it. Receive God's grace so you can be a grace-giver.

God Isn't Keeping A Record Of Your Wrongs

The purpose of your problems is to recognize that you will always need God's grace. But there's another reason you need to understand the purpose of your problems. In Psalm 130:3, it says, "If you, Lord, kept a record of my sins, who could stand?"

He isn't keeping a record of your wrongs—and therefore, neither should you.

These are the words of a man who understands just how much he sins, and how much grace God extended to him.

Another reason God allows problems is to teach you that He isn't keeping a record of your wrongs—and therefore, *neither should you.* Remember what the Lord says: "Just as I forgive you, you should forgive others."

Don't focus on your problem. Focus on what Jesus Christ has done for you.

A lot of the time, the first thing we do when we're in the pit crying out to God because of our problem is to ask God, "What did I do wrong?" But God says He isn't keeping a record of your sins. He's using your problem to remind you of what He has done right.

God wants you to recognize that whether you're in a low place or a high place in your life, the purpose of your problem is not to keep a record of your sins. *Don't focus on your problem. Focus on what Jesus Christ has done for you.*

See, if God did not erase the sins that you entered into willingly and ignorantly, if He did not throw those sins into the sea of forgetfulness and allow His blood to wash and cleanse you, then you wouldn't have a chance. None of us would. We'd be destined for hell with no chance of reconciliation or redemption.

That is why you must see that you always need the grace of God.

Psalm 130:4 says: "But with you, Lord, there is forgiveness so that we can with reverence serve you."

There is forgiveness with the Lord. Why? So you can serve Him with reverence. Reverence means to express a loving fear, to be in awe of. Reverence will lead you into a deeper level of worship as well. This is very important!

If you haven't been worshiping God in your problem—and I know I'm guilty of this; nobody feels like worshipping during a problem or making a joyful noise—you must recognize that worshiping Him is *exactly* what He wants you to do.

Until we learn how important it is to serve Him in spite of our problems, we'll never understand that our problems have purpose.

Dive into that place of worship. When you feel weak, God says you're strong. Allow your spirit to control your emotions. Don't allow your problems to control your emotions. Your spirit says, *let's worship and cry and praise.* Your emotion says, *let's focus on the problem and worry.*

Revere Him. Worship Him. Magnify Him. Exalt Him. Lift up His name and declare the Lord as your Savior and Deliverer. Don't succumb to the emotions that want to take over your vocal cords like a sickness, plague you. Instead, out of the depth of your pain, cry out how great God is.

Do it right now, if the Spirit moves. Cry out to God. Tell Him you'll love Him no matter where you are or what you're going through.

Read the rest of Psalm 130:4: "But with you, Lord, there is forgiveness so that we can with reverence serve you."

In the midst of your sorrow, do you still serve God? Even though you've fallen, God still says, *Serve Me.* Even in your brokenness, a bad marriage, a dysfunctional relationship, God still doesn't give you an excuse _not_ to serve Him. Before you can say it, NO, it's not fair, but it's not about being fair, it's about God being just! He says, "In spite of what you're going through, worship and serve Me."

Why? Because God is great. And until you learn how important it is to serve Him in spite of your problems, you'll never understand that your problems have purpose.

And your problems definitely have purpose. God only allows things to happen that bring Him honor and glory. Don't believe me? Check out Romans 8:28: "All things work together for the good to those who love the Lord; who are called according to his purpose." The question is, *Do you know who you are?*

CHAPTER FOUR

Know Who You Are And Live With Purpose

*Now a man named Lazarus was sick. He was from Bethany, the village of Mary and her sister Martha. (This Mary, whose brother Lazarus now lay sick, was the same one who poured perfume on the Lord and wiped his feet with her hair). So the sisters sent word to Jesus, 'Lord, the one you love is sick.' When he heard this, Jesus said, 'This sickness will not end in death. No, it is for God's glory so that God's Son may be glorified through it.' Now Jesus loved Martha and her sister and Lazarus. So when he heard that Lazarus was sick, he stayed where he was two more days.' — **John 11:1-6***

In this passage, we have a problem involving a family: Mary, Martha and Lazarus, three siblings that Jesus loved.

Lazarus, the brother, had fallen sick with a life-threatening illness, and his sisters had an expectation. They were hoping God would do something for their brother.

By now, you're probably expecting something too. You may have a problem right now, whether it's financial, relational, mental, or something in your family or your job. And I'm glad you have an expectation. In fact, let me ask you this: What is your expectation of God right now? What are you hoping He will do for you?

If you're going to understand the purpose of your problem, you must understand the difference between *existing* and *living*. Ask these questions of yourself:

- Who am I?

- What am I here for?

- What does God want to do with me?

If you don't understand the purpose of your life and the reason God created you, you'll never understand the difference between existing and living.

A person who's existing is just here. They inhale and exhale; they go about life. But a person who is living has *purpose*. They know who they are, they know why they exist, and they know what God is up to in their life.

Are you willing to go through whatever problems God allows in your life in order to bring you to the place he wants you to be?

You're not really living until you know the correct answers to the questions above, and live a life that reflects it. A lot of people have problems because they don't know these things in their heart. They're living to die instead of dying to live.

Make no mistake. Even people who are living on purpose have problems. The difference is they know and recognize that every problem in their life contributes to their purpose.

When you don't know your purpose, your problems take advantage of you. They control you and beat you down to the point where you want to kill yourself.

The challenge of your life is this: Are you willing to go through whatever problems God allows in your life in order to bring you to the place He wants you to be?

I want you to see something happening in John 11: "When he heard that Lazarus was sick, He stayed where He was two more days."

Normally when someone is sick, you rush to that person's bedside because that's what you feel you need to do. But when Jesus received word of Lazarus, He chose to stay where He was for two more days. And notice what He said in the text in verse four: "This sickness will not end in death. No, it is for God's glory so that God's Son may be glorified through it."

Stop and remember this afresh: *Whatever I'm going through, it's for God's glory.* Your problem has a purpose, and everything on earth, everything in heaven, and everything in hell will bring God glory. Make this your mindset. Say to yourself: *No matter what I'm dealing with, no matter what I'm going through, no matter how*

*painful it is, I'm committed Lord for your glory. I'd ra-
ther have problems that glorify You than no problems
and glorifying myself!*

Risk It All To Save Somebody Else

John 11:7-13 says, "Then he said to his disciples, 'Let us
go back to Judea.' 'But Rabbi,' they said, 'a short while
ago the Jews tried to stone you and yet you are going
back there?' And Jesus said, 'Are there not 12 hours of
daylight? A man who walks by day will not stumble for
he sees by this world's light. It is when he walks by night
that he stumbles for he has no light.' After he had said
this he went on to tell them, 'Our friend Lazarus has fall-
en asleep but I am going there to wake him up.' His
disciples replied, 'Lord if he is sleeping he will get better.'"

*Are you willing to go through whatev-
er problems God allows in your life in
order to bring you to the place He
wants you to be?*

Jesus had been speaking of Lazarus' death but His
disciples thought He meant natural sleep. Going to Judea
meant going to the place where the Pharisees and Saddu-
cees wanted to kill Jesus too.

Now let me ask you: When was the last time you put
yourself at risk for another person's problem? When was
the last time you were prepared to sacrifice yourself?

I don't mean to the point of death, but not excluding
it. But when was the last time you were willing to put

yourself at the great risk of sacrificing everything about you for the benefit of somebody else? Because when you understand that your problems have purpose, sometimes you're going to have to risk it all in order to save somebody else from their problems.

Others Will Recognize How Good God Is

You may be wondering: *Where is Jesus in my problem? Why didn't He show up during my horrible divorce? During my horrible breakup? During that time I lost my job and couldn't find an apartment? I've been praying, fasting, and pleading, but where is He?*

Here's the thing: Jesus hasn't come because bailing you out too early would hurt you, not help you.

The purpose of your problem is so that others can recognize how good God is.

God, being the God He is, understands that your problems have purpose. He understands that He has to let certain things play out even though it hurts. Otherwise the purpose will never be fulfilled in your problem. And if it's not fulfilled, you'll miss out on learning a lesson in your life and bringing glory to God.

There are some people who will never believe in the power of God until they see you rescued from your problem. Your problem is what will introduce them to God. In other words, the purpose of your problem is so that others can recognize how good God is.

Ask yourself: *Am I going to complain about my problem, or am I going to allow the purpose of my problem to run its course that God might be glorified through the belief of another?*

When God Doesn't Show Up

In John 11:17-22, Lazarus has been dead for four days because Jesus stayed where He was for two days and then traveled two more days to Jerusalem.

Many Jews had come to comfort Mary and Martha and mourn with them in the loss of their brother. When Martha heard Jesus was coming, she went to meet Him, but Mary stayed home.

Martha said to Jesus, "Lord, if you had been here my brother would not have died. But I know that even now God will give you whatever you ask."

And Jesus said to her: "Your brother will rise again."

Even though God doesn't show up when you think you need Him, He shows up exactly when He needs to be there.

Because the custom was to bury the dead within 24 hours, Jesus had missed the funeral. Have you felt like that with your problem? Like God didn't show up to the funeral of your problem? He didn't show up the day you died in your marriage, the day your divorce papers were finalized, the day your girlfriend or boyfriend left you, the day your car was repossessed, the day your car broke down and you didn't have money to get it fixed. Have you been there before?

Why? Why didn't God show up? Because your problem has a purpose.

Here's what you have to realize: Even though God doesn't show up when you think you need Him, He shows up exactly when He needs to be there.

If you want to understand the purpose of your problem, you must learn to look to Jesus as the source of your deliverance.

Consider John 11: 23-35: "After Martha had spoken to Jesus, He replied to her: 'Your brother will rise again.'"

In verse 24, Martha replies, "I know he will rise again in the resurrection at the last day."

But Jesus says in verse 25, "I am the resurrection and the life. He who believes in me will live, even though he dies." Then He says in verse 26 that whoever believes in Him will *never* die. That's not a tongue twister out of Green Eggs and Ham. This is straight out of the Holy Bible.

Do you believe this? Do you believe Christ? Do you believe God is in control of what's going on around you, even if you're hurting from it? Do you believe that, regardless of what you've gone through as a child and adult—even horrible things—that God is still in control?

Do you believe that yes, your problem has a purpose, and that God understands the purpose of that problem? Do you believe God has a plan for you in spite of what you've been through? Do you believe the plan God has for you will trump the amount of pain you've been dealing with, and bring you to a place where God is glorified?

Your Problems Point Others to Christ

People are going to believe in Jesus Christ because of you. People are going to have a deeper walk with Him because of what you've been through. Do you believe this?

So don't focus on your problem. Focus on how your problem can point someone to Christ. How? By elevating your thinking. When you elevate your thinking, you eliminate the pain in your problem.

It's like getting on an airplane. While you're on the runway, you see everything up-close. But once that plane takes off, the world below seems smaller and smaller.

When your thinking is too low, your problems dictate your life. You haven't elevated your mind high enough.

Take a look at your problems while seated next to God. Trust me, you won't even recognize them. They'll be too small for the naked eye. So look to Jesus as the source of your deliverance. Believe that He is the Resurrection and the Life. Leave behind all the excuses that are separating you from God.

Look at John 11:27-31: "'Yes, Lord,' Martha told him, 'I believe that you are the Christ, the Son of God, who is come into the world.' And after she had said this, she went back and she called her sister Mary. 'The Teacher is here,' she said, 'and he is asking for you.' When Mary heard this, she got up quickly and she went to him. Now Jesus had not yet entered the village, but was still at the place where Martha had met him. When the Jews who had been with Mary in the house, comforting her, noticed how quickly she got up and went out, they followed her, supposing she was going to the tomb to mourn there."

Mary was broken and tattered, mourning the death of her brother. But as soon as she heard that Jesus was nearby, she immediately got up and took off running.

Jesus is always nearby. Run to Him. Leave your problem and run to Him. How do you run to Jesus? Metaphorically speaking, you run straight for a mirror. Because baby when you stand in front of a mirror, you'll find Him because He's inside of you. You run to Jesus with your heart not with your feet – PRAY! As soon as you act on your faith and begin to pray… "Father in the name of Jesus…" you're in His presence and He and you know everything is going to be alright.

If You Believe, You Will See God's Glory

In John 11:32, when Mary reached the place where Jesus was, she fell at his feet and said, "Lord, if you had been here, my brother would not have died." Notice, that's the same thing her sister said.

When Jesus saw her weeping, He was deeply moved in his spirit. Then He said, "Where have you laid him?"

They replied, "Come and see, Lord."

When you remove your dead doubt, God can remove your dead problem.

John 11:35 is the shortest verse in the Bible: "Jesus wept." Then in verse 36, the Jews wept and said, "See how he loved him!" But some of them said, "Could not he who opened the eyes of the blind man have kept this man from dying?"

In other words, they questioned Jesus.

But then Jesus came to the cave and said, "Take away the stone."

"But, Lord," said Martha, the sister of the dead man, "by this time there is a bad odor, for he has been in there for four days."

Then Jesus said, "Didn't I tell you that if you believe, you will see the glory of God?"

So they took away the stone. And Jesus looked up and said, "Father, I thank you that you have heard me. I knew that you always hear me, but I said this for the benefit of the people standing here, that they may believe that you sent me."

Never Doubt God's Methods

Living in doubt robs God of His glory. Everyone warned Jesus not to take away the stone because of the smell. But He didn't care. He had that stone of doubt rolled away.

When you remove your dead doubt, God can remove your dead problem. Once you do, that's when you'll understand the purpose of your problem.

You may have been through something horrible, been laid off, molested, raped, fatherless, abused, addicted, the mother or father of a child going off the deep end. But these are not excuses and should not be an excuse for the purpose of your problem NOT being fulfilled in your life.

Finally, take off things that represent your past situation. Look at John 11:43: "When he had said this, Jesus called in a loud voice, 'Lazarus, come out!' The dead man came out, his hands and feet wrapped with strips of linen, and a cloth around his face. Jesus said to them, 'Take off the thing that he no longer needs. Take off the grave clothes and let him go.'"

Take off your past situation. Take off the grave clothes. Take off the pain and doubt you keep rehearsing in your mind about your problem.

What dead things do you need to remove right now from your life? Take them off. You don't need them anymore.

Peel them off by opening your mouth and saying, "Lord, I take off my problems and put on purpose. I take off sorrow and put on joy. I take off hate and put on love. I take off chaos and wear peace. I take off impatience and put on patience. I choose to walk in your Spirit so I will not fulfill the lust of my flesh."

Look to Jesus as the source of your deliverance. Take away the excuses that are separating you from God. Do this, and you will understand the purpose of your problems even though you're still broken!

CHAPTER FIVE

Accept The Fact That Brokenness Hurts

He heals the brokenhearted and binds up their wounds.' —
Psalm 147:3

When you think about your problem, do you ask yourself:

- "How did I ever get myself into this situation?"

- "How did I become so vulnerable?"

- "How did I allow my guards to be lowered so far?"

- "How did I not see this coming?"

These questions bring us to a very important question right now: *What do you do now?*

Here you are. You've got a problem, you don't understand its purpose, you're struggling in your walk. And now you need to figure out what to do about it and how you can get above and beyond this situation.

Time doesn't heal all wounds. Time dates all wounds. Forgiveness heals.

This is where to start: *Lord, I need your help.* That's what you must pray.

Then it's time to let the tears come. It's time to let the guilt fade. It's time to forgive. Time doesn't heal all wounds. Time dates all wounds. Forgiveness heals.

You might have been haunted by your problems for a long time. Maybe you've dealt with it for years, for generations. Your problems haunt you everywhere you go. You can't shake it, can't get away from it. You don't feel God in your situation even though you pray, fast, and ask Him to remove the problem.

Brokenness hurts. Emotionally, spiritually, and psychologically. You feel alone and isolated, even if you're in a crowded room.

You have a real problem that produces real pain.

But it also has a very real purpose.

There's purpose in feeling insignificant. There's purpose in feeling empty. There's purpose in depression, addiction, persistent shame, obsessive thoughts, compulsive behaviors, and struggles with perfectionism.

I like what Dr. Richard Swenson said in his book, *A Minute of Margin*: "Broken relationships are a razor across the artery of the spirit. Stemming the hemorrhage and binding the wound should be done as quickly as possible. Yet all too often it takes months or years and sometimes the bleeding never stops."

Are You Wearing A Mask?

Many of us have emotional bleeding. But we can't stop it because it's on the inside. So we wear masks so people don't know we have a problem. We go to church and someone asks, "Hey brother, how you doing?"

We all know how to camouflage our pain in public.

Then we respond, "Praise the Lord, I'm blessed and highly favored."

We know how to say the right things, walk the walk, lift up holy hands, *hem* and *haw*, do the handshake, give the church hug, read Scripture with power and authority.

But it's all camouflage. We all know how to camouflage our pain in public.

So here's the issue we have: If you don't accept the fact that brokenness hurts, you'll never discover the real purpose.

Are You Trying To Ease Your Pain With Addictions?

When you don't know the purpose of your problem, you usually use a harmful substance to ease the pain (i.e. sex, drugs, alcohol, gambling, food, etc.).

When you treat your problem with these painful substances, they numb you. After a while, you can't feel the pain of what you're going through because you have medicated it. Some of you have been in so much pain that you didn't even realize you were in pain. You were anesthetized ... unable to feel the pain but definitely not free from the pain!

And so when you took this painful substance it just made the circumstance or the situation worse. Your problem worsened. It's like you're on fire but you don't know it.

And you know what happens when you're on fire and don't know it? You're going to let the fire burn until it scorches your body so badly that it kills you.

But if you know you're on fire, you have a chance to put it out.

Only God Can Heal Your Brokenness

You might be thinking, *I'm the one who's using sex, food, drugs, alcohol, and gambling to numb my pain. I'm the one who thinks my life is insignificant. I'm the one who has excessive anxiety. I'm the one who's bitter. I'm the one who's depressed and has several addictions. I'm the one who has persistent shame. So what now?*

You need to understand that only God can heal your brokenness.

You've been trying to heal your brokenness in so many ways that just don't work, and because you've been enamored by your pain for so long, you don't think God can understand where you are, or fix the pain you're contending with.

But remember: "The Lord heals the brokenhearted and He binds up their wounds."

See, when you understand that only God can heal your brokenness, when you understand that only God can relate to your pain, when you understand a Savior went to the cross for you ... you start to see purpose in your problem.

Christ alone brings closure to your problem. Not the guy or girl you broke up with, not anyone. It's Christ alone that closes the door to pain and opens the door to glory. I believe William McDowell said, "Once you can give yourself away, closure comes with Christ.

In other words, once you accept that Jesus has a purpose for your life, you can get the closure you need in the painful area of your life. If you accept Jesus is the way, the truth, and the life, then you'll discover closure.

Those who never experience closure are those who cannot accept that God has a purpose for their problem. So don't rule God out of your problem, even though you're going through hell. You have to come to the conclusion that God is involved in what you're dealing with—He's your heavenly Father and He cares!

Love God More Than Your Pain

When it comes to your pain, don't say, "I guess this is the life God wants me to live, a life of pain." No, that's not how it works. You need to understand that God wants you to love Him more than you love your pain. That may sound strange about loving your pain, but sometimes people become so comfortable in their painful situation that they see it as their purpose. This isn't right. Your life has purpose, and that purpose isn't a life of pain. Instead, you need to turn to God and say, "I love you more than what I'm going through. I embrace you where I am. I'm not going to get comfortable in my problem."

The Bible says that God is near to the brokenhearted, and that He saves those who are crushed in spirit, and binds up their wounds (Psalm 34:18).

The Bible also says that God is the potter, and we are the clay. And it's in our brokenness that God does His best work. You still don't believe me and you're wondering what can God do with my broken, messed up self and better yet, why would He want me? What purpose could possibly be in this daughter of dysfunction, this son of sadness? Here it is, the purpose of your problem is so that God can get His hands on you, on your brokenness, so He can fix it! Jesus said it like this, "I came for those who were sick, not well!" (Luke 5:31).

The pain you're struggling with right now? God has allowed it so that you will learn to let Him get His hands on you. You see, as long as we're broken, we keep running to God in prayer, in praise, and in seeking Him.

God oftentimes will allow problems in our lives so that you will maintain a dependence upon Him. In other words, the purpose of the problem is so that you will have a dependence upon God. If He delivered you from all of your problems, He knows that you would feel no reason to need Him.

God wants you. A relationship with you. But for some—and this may be you—we only relate to God when we're in trouble.

Just look at your life right now. Are you closer to God because of what you're dealing with? Do you think about Him more often? Talk to Him?

What would you be like if He removed the problems? Would you still be the person God's called you to be? Would you still pray like you pray and praise like you praise? Would you still seek God?

You don't know the answer, and neither do I. But God does.

And He will do what He must to keep His hands on you. Now, all you have to do is what you must to keep your eyes on Him. How? Simply ask the question, "What is the purpose of my problems?"

CHAPTER SIX

Ask God What The Purpose Of Your Problem Is

God is our refuge and strength, an ever-present help in trouble. — **Psalm 46:1**

Sometimes we don't understand why our problems tend to get the best of us. We don't understand why God allows these problems in our lives. Especially for that person who has been praying, praising, and not allowing their problem to get the best of them.

You believe you've done everything that God has asked you to do. You did it with purpose, with intent, and with a glad heart while trusting the Lord.

But you still can't seem to be able to harvest from your sacrifices. You're putting in time, energy and effort into serving God, the Kingdom, blessing your pastor and the people of your church and community, and being gracious at work and at school and with your neighbors, and loving your enemies … *so what's wrong?*

Then the enemy comes along and tries to fill you with doubt and unbelief. Like John the Baptist, you're in prison—problems having gotten the best of you—and you're experiencing doubt, wondering if Jesus is who He said He was.

When you discover the purpose of your problem, you begin to understand what role it plays in your destiny.

Sometimes you get to a place in your life where you just can't seem to understand. You find yourself thinking: *What's going on, God? I'm in the dark, yet I'm in the light. What are you doing? I know I'm in fellowship with You, but I just can't seem to understand any of this.*

Instead of fretting, you must ask: *What purpose does this problem have in my life, Lord?*

Sometimes, you have to go after the problem. You have to find it. Because it's possible you've been running from it so long that it has become a coping mechanism that you can't even see. So you have to find it. Grab it by the collar. Look it in the face and say, "What do you want with me? What's your purpose in my life?"

God will answer that question for you. He will make that problem speak up.

When you discover the purpose of your problem, you begin to understand what role it plays in your destiny.

Don't Let Your Life Go In Circles

See, you're trying to get somewhere. God has placed all of us on a divine path called destiny. And sometimes we just let our life go in a circle. You walk around and around, not knowing where you're going. And all this time you've been missing out on the fact that your problem can be a great pointer.

Problems will point you in the right direction. They'll tell you where to go.

A lot of us have been blessed because of a mess.

Some of us know where not to go because we've been there and didn't like it. So you think, "Problem, thank you for showing me where I shouldn't have been in the first place." That problem pointed you in the right direction.

Some of us have to understand that if our problems had not rejected us, we would have never been able to get into a place called the blessing. A lot of us have been blessed because of a mess. We were going in the wrong direction, doing the wrong things, hanging out with the wrong people. And God dropped that problem into our laps so it would point us right to Him.

Whenever you are faced with problems, never run to a place that you can't trust.

Check out Psalm 46:1. God is our *refuge*. That word means hiding place. So when a tornado comes through, the sirens go off and you run to the refuge, the hiding place, the hide out that's strong enough to handle the turbulence that's coming from the storm.

Maybe this describes you today. You refuse to run, thinking you can handle the destruction. Or you run to a place that's not strong enough to handle the storm. In other words, you run to a place that cannot be trusted.

Trust means to have a firm reliance on the integrity or the ability or the character of a person or thing.

To run to your refuge is to look for God. It's a good time to start worshipping, praying, and saying, "Lord, I love You, I praise You, I magnify You. God, You are real, You're awesome, You're magnificent, my Wonderful Counselor and Everlasting Father."

A lot of us are getting beat up by our problems because we run to a place that cannot be trusted and we haven't learned to praise God in the midst of the problem.

I want to make sure you understand exactly what the word *trust* really means.

Trust means to have a firm reliance on the integrity or the ability or the character of a person or thing.

In other words, you can trust God.

Watch Out For Stubbornness

Some of us are just too stubborn to go to the refuge of God. We're as stiff as a mule. We hear that when we're in a problem, all we have to do is pray and praise. But that's too easy.

You might be in a hurricane in your life right now, being tossed to and fro. You're being spun around and you're dizzy. Your situation is just so messed up.

But thanks be to God that you can trust Him. God has never let you down. It's impossible. He will never leave you, nor forsake you. He is your refuge today, yesterday, and tomorrow.

How Can You Trust The Place You're In?

You're probably wondering how you can know whether or not you can trust the problem you're in. How can you be sure of the integrity, ability, and character of the place you're in?

It's simple. Ask yourself this one question: *Is God there?*

If God is, where are you? If you know you ran to a place where God is, then you know and can trust that place.

Now, I can hear you thinking right now, hear your spirit crying out with this question: *How can I know if God is there or not?* That's a great question.

Answer: You know God is there if by faith you trust Him enough to invite Him in!

God won't always make your problem go away, but He will always go through your problem with you.

If you pray, then God will come to your aid. If you praise Him, He will come to your aid. If you worship Him, He will come to your aid.

Hear this: If you worship God in spirit and in truth, He will always show up. That's how you know if God is where you are.

God manifests His presence every single time. So the best way to get out of a problem is to worship. If you begin to worship God in spirit and in truth, He will show up. And you better believe that if He doesn't make the problem go away, that you can handle it *with* Him.

God won't always make your problem go away, but He will always go through your problem with you. And if God is going through your problem with you, it doesn't matter what you're going through.

- It doesn't matter what your doctor said.

- It doesn't matter what your friend did to you.

- It doesn't matter how your children are behaving.

- It doesn't matter if your husband or wife left you.

- It doesn't matter if your cat died.

- It doesn't matter if your car was repossessed.

- It doesn't matter if your house was foreclosed.

- It doesn't matter if you were kicked out of school.

If God is for you, who can be against you? Run to Him.

Psalm 9:9-10 says: *"The Lord is a refuge for the oppressed, a stronghold in times of trouble. Those who know your name trust in you, for you, Lord, have never forsaken those who seek you."*

Whenever you have problems, never depend on your own strength.

There is power in the name of Jesus. There is deliverance in Jesus. There is healing in Jesus. Demons tremble at His name. When you know the name of Jesus, and rely on Him, it puts you in a position where you can say, "I trust in the Lord with all my heart. I lean not on my own understanding. In all my ways, I acknowledge Him and He directs my path."

Yes, the Lord will order your steps.

Problems Introduce You To Jesus

A lot of people would never discover who God is until their problems introduced them to Him. This is amazing to think about. Just think through the ramifications.

This means we can't get to know God just by reading the Word. We can't get to know God by simply going to church. We can't get to know God just by listening to songs of adoration and songs of praise.

A lot of us would never meet Him until our problems spoke up, saying, "I'm your problem and I'd like to introduce you to Jesus." A lot of us would never get to know God beyond His name if our problem didn't take us into a deeper realm with Him. That's another purpose for your problem.

Never Depend Upon Your Own Strength

Whenever you have problems, never depend on your own strength.

Remember Psalm 46? God is your refuge and strength. He's your ever-present help in trouble.

If you try to shoulder your problem by yourself, the weight is enough to kill you. You don't have the strength to sustain your problems. See, problems will always drain you of your strength. They will pull your life essence out of you. Never depend upon your own strength when you are faced with problems.

You're not strong enough to handle life independent of God. The purpose of your problem is to get you in the spiritual weight room called dependence, trust, and reliance.

When you're getting on your knees, praying, and totally depending on God for everything in your life, that's when you're strong.

Look at 2 Corinthians 12:8-10: *"Three different times I begged the Lord to take it away. Each time he said, 'My grace is all you need. My power works best in weakness.' So now I am glad to boast about my weaknesses, so that the power of Christ can work through me. That's why I take pleasure in my weaknesses, and in the insults, hardships, persecutions, and troubles that I suffer for Christ. For when I am weak, then I am strong."*

When you have problems in your life, it all comes down to how you look at them.

According to the Word of God, when your problem shows up, the power of God shows up. Now that's a tradeoff. I don't know what you've got going on in your life, but, the more hell released against you on earth, the more God's power is going to be released in your life (even if you don't recognize it). And the only way you're going to recognize it is to do what Paul did: Begin to boast.

Brag gladly about your weaknesses. Delight in your insults and hardships. Take pleasure in your persecutions and difficulty. Why? Because when you have problems, you have strength!

The purpose of your problem is to introduce you to God's power, and that's what you've been missing. God's power can't rest on you until you embrace the fact that your problem has a purpose in your life, and once you realize this, the floodgates of Heaven release its rain, says Bishop Paul Morton.

When God's power shows up, deliverance shows up. When deliverance shows up, it cleans house. It changes your perspective. It directs your thoughts from your problem to your God.

Don't depend on the strength of your finances, your marriage, or your current relationship. You can only rely on the strength of God.

God says He is ever-present. Your problems may have snuck up on you, but they didn't sneak up on God. He saw your problems coming before you were born. And He knew He'd be there with you.

At the end of the day, your problems don't have power over you. You don't have to worry because it has already been defeated. God says you don't have to get bent out of shape, because He's already taken your problem to the cross. When Jesus went to the cross, He said, "It is finished."

What was finished? Your problem.

Even molestation? Finished.

Even rape? Finished.

Even divorce? Finished.

Even the death of my loved one? Finished.

It doesn't matter what your problem is. Jesus says, "I got it. I took your problem. I dealt with it."

Run To The Word Of God

You always have a solution to your problem: The Word of God. The only way a problem will ever be able to take advantage of you is if you don't know the Word.

When your problem shows up, God says, "I'm always here." So don't forget that God is your refuge, your hiding place, your strength, your power, your ever-present help in time of trouble.

Your problems will try to make you feel like God has abandoned you. But it's impossible. *Impossible.* God won't ever leave you. If you're born again and have accepted Jesus Christ as your Lord and Savior, then it's impossible for God to ever leave you. Because you are the temple of the Holy Spirit. Where you are, God is. Let that sink in. Let that stick.

You might say, where was God when I went through this horrible problem? But He was right there. He didn't let your problem kill you. He didn't let your problem drive you crazy. God let you survive. And even though you were hurt, God made you stronger through it. He formed your testimony to be someone else's deliverance.

Sometimes the reason God lets your problem crush you is so He can put you back together again.

Take a moment right now. Say, "Father, whatever you're doing in this season of my life, I want to be in it with you. I want to trust you."

Consider Hebrews 11:6 in the Message Translation: "It's impossible to please God apart from faith. And why? Because anyone who wants to approach God must believe both that he exists *and* that he cares enough to respond to those who seek him."

Now check out Psalm 34:18: "The Lord is close to the brokenhearted; he rescues those whose spirits are crushed."

Are you crushed in spirit? Are you under the foot of the enemy? Are you under the foot of finances, broken relationships, alcohol, drugs, rejection, abandonment?

God is saying to you, "Listen. I am close to you. I will save you. I will mend your spirit."

Sometimes the reason God lets your problem crush you is so He can put you back together again. And if God goes through the motions of putting you back together again, the last thing He wants you to do is to let your problems have power over you!

CHAPTER SEVEN

Find Victory In Your Problems

Therefore, since through God's mercy we have this minis-
try, we do not lose heart. Rather, we have renounced secret
and shameful ways; we do not use deception, nor do we
distort the word of God. On the contrary, by setting forth
the truth plainly we commend ourselves to everyone's con-
science in the sight of God. And even if our gospel is
veiled, it is veiled to those who are perishing. The god of
this age has blinded the minds of unbelievers, so that they
cannot see the light of the gospel that displays the glory of
Christ, who is the image of God. For what we preach is not
ourselves, but Jesus Christ as Lord, and ourselves as your
servants for Jesus' sake. For God, who said, 'Let light
shine out of darkness,' made his light shine in our hearts to
give us the light of the knowledge of God's glory displayed
in the face of Christ. But we have this treasure in jars of
clay to show that this all-surpassing power is from
God and not from us. We are hard pressed on every
side, but not crushed; perplexed, but not in des-
pair; persecuted, but not abandoned; struck down, but not
destroyed. We always carry around in our body the death
of Jesus, so that the life of Jesus may also be revealed in
our body. For we who are alive are always being given
over to death for Jesus' sake, so that his life may also be
revealed in our mortal body. So then, death is at work in
us, but life is at work in you. It is written: 'I believed;
therefore I have spoken.' Since we have that same spirit

of faith, we also believe and therefore speak, because we know that the one who raised the Lord Jesus from the dead will also raise us with Jesus and present us with you to himself. All this is for your benefit, so that the grace that is reaching more and more people may cause thanksgiving to overflow to the glory of God. Therefore we do not lose heart. Though outwardly we are wasting away, yet inwardly we are being renewed day by day. For our light and momentary troubles are achieving for us an eternal glory that far outweighs them all. So we fix our eyes not on what is seen, but on what is unseen, since what is seen is temporary, but what is unseen is eternal. — 2 Corinthians 4:1-18

What does this passage mean for us today? What does it mean for your problem? What does it mean for your purpose?

Well, let's let the Bible speak for itself. Let's identify the problem that's in this text and figure out what's really going on and how it relates to us. And then let us apply it to our lives and discover how to contend with the problems.

Let me say this first: No matter what's going on in your life, no matter what negative thing has shown up on your doorstep, no matter what problem keeps bugging you, you still have the power of decision over how you feel about it. That can never be taken from you.

Say you go to a doctor and get bad news. You still have a choice. The doctor may have diagnosed something happening with you, but you are the one who gets to determine how you feel about it.

Just because your husband or wife says, "I want a divorce," does not mandate how you feel. Just because one of your children has been disrespectful or rebellious does not mandate how you feel. Problems do not have the power to make you feel a certain way.

Now, don't get me wrong. When something bad happens that you don't like, you have a right to get angry. Even God says, "Be angry and sin not."

But here's the thing: Just because you're angry or disappointed doesn't mean you let it control you.

Take Control Of Your Feelings

Whenever a problem shows up in your life, the first thing you must recognize is that the thing you're dealing with has a purpose in your life. And so you have to sit back and grab control of your feelings, bring them under arrest. Ponder. Meditate. Know this to be true. Start a conversation with God, and do not allow your feelings to control you.

You need to know that God is in control of your circumstances—but He is not in control of your feelings. Now, just the fact that God allowed it doesn't mean He initiated it. But if He allowed it to come into your life, you've got to understand that He is in control, just not of your feelings.

God is not a puppeteer. He's not a master robot controller in the sky. God has given you something that He desires for you to give back to Him: free will. He's given you free will so that you would freely choose Him and freely walk in obedience to Him, even when He allows problems to come into your life.

> *Once you've learned the purpose in your problem, then God removes the problem from your life.*

See, if God has allowed it, then there's a purpose to it, and a benefit to it. It will make you better, make you stronger, bring you closer to God and teach you to pray. It will encourage you and build you up to make you the right person at the right time so that, when a problem shows up again in the life of another person, you are right there to contend with it.

Your Problem Is For Your Benefit

Once you've learned the purpose in your problem, then God removes the problem from your life.

See, once you discover the purpose of your problem, you begin to live your life in deliverance from it. You begin to live above the problem. In other words, the problem takes its rightful position: Under your feet.

But this might not be where you're at right now.

> *But know this: The only people who get angry at God are people who don't understand the purpose of the problem.*

Your problem may be lasting for weeks, months, years because you won't sit down long enough to discover the purpose of it. You keep complaining about the problem instead of complying with the will of God to determine what God is up to!

This isn't to make light of your pain at all. You may feel like God is not listening to you throughout your problem. You may get angry at God, which I really do not recommend (just read Job).

But know this: The only people who get angry at God are people who don't understand the purpose of the problem.

If you don't understand the purpose of your problem, you will get angry at God. You're going to say, "What kind of God would let this happen?" You'll begin to question His integrity.

If this is where you're at, take a moment and repent. Say, "God, I'm so sorry. I was caught up in my flesh with my feelings, and I tried to blame you."

Thanksgiving That Overflows To The Lord

In 2 Corinthians 4:8, we see that we are hard pressed on every side but we're not crushed. We are perplexed, but we are not in despair. Let's take a look at this. You might find yourself in this place.

You're confused, though not in despair. You're being persecuted right now, maybe by your wife, or husband, or friends, or boyfriend, or girlfriend, or boss, or manager. But check this out: You're not abandoned. You're being struck down, but you're not destroyed.

What is the purpose of all this? It's for your benefit. It doesn't matter what has happened to you. You have to come to the conclusion that if God allowed it, it's for your benefit. Check out verse 15 in 2 Corinthians 4: "All this is for your benefit, so that the grace that is reaching more and more people may cause thanksgiving to overflow to the glory of God."

Beyond Your Natural Eyes

Now catch this: You will not be able to see the benefit of your problem through your natural eyes. It's impossible. The only way you're going to be able to conclude that the problem in your life has a benefit is if you get a revelation of who God is. Your flesh doesn't have the ability to comprehend the benefit of pain. Your flesh only wants to get away from pain.

Your flesh says, *Stop. I don't like this. It hurts.*

Let me ask you this now: What are you going through? What are you contending with? What are you hiding? What are you trying to avoid? What is it that you have been going through that has brought you to tears? What has brought you into a state of depression? What are you dealing with that won't let you sleep? What is causing you nightmares? What has you sitting in front of a psychiatrist? What has you in a hospital? What has you stressed? What has you screaming at those you love?

How is this for your benefit? Remember 2 Corinthians 4:15? It says: "All this is for your benefit, so that the grace that is reaching more and more people may cause thanksgiving to overflow to the glory of God."

The writer is saying that what you're going through is for your benefit, even though it's painful and perplexing. But God has not abandoned you, friend.

You may be thrown down, rejected, and abandoned by people. But the God of the universe says it's for your benefit because more and more people are giving thanks and glory to God.

Your Problems Are Momentary Afflictions

Look at 2 Corinthians 4:16-18: "Therefore we do not lose heart. Though outwardly we are wasting away, yet inwardly we are being renewed day by day. For our light and momentary troubles are achieving for us an eternal glory that far outweighs them all. So we fix our eyes not on what is seen, but on what is unseen, since what is seen is temporary, but what is unseen is eternal."

That is amazing. That is spectacular! If you don't get anything from this book, just get that.

If you're weighed down with a spirit of heaviness, depression, despair, despondency, God says that it is a momentary problem that is achieving eternal glory that far outweighs the pain of it.

Remember ever playing on a see-saw? You go up, down, up, down, up, down. But here's the thing: Whoever was the heaviest or whoever knew how to shift their weight just the right way was able to control the individual on the other end.

God's glory is the heavy side here. It is so much heavier than the problems that are going to be dangling in the air the entire time, helpless.

This is what God is saying to your problems: "Don't ever get into a battle with me, because you'll always lose. You're too light and too momentary."

Fix Your Eyes On Eternal Glory

In 2 Corinthians 4:18, God says fix your eyes not on what you *can* see, but what you *can't* see, because what you can't see is eternal.

Don't look at what's going to evaporate. Look at what will last forever. Focus on your faith. Focus on what God has done for you.

Don't get things mixed up. Don't say that you have to see before you believe. Believe before you see. That's when you see through the eyes of God, and are not easily swayed by things right in front of you.

Repeat this to yourself: *What I am going through is temporary. What I am going through is too light to handle me. What I am going through is momentary. What I am going through doesn't have the capacity to contend with the glory that's on the inside of me bursting in thanksgiving to God.*

You know that time you texted and drove at the same time? Pretty much everyone has at some point. Maybe all you were going to text was, "K," but when you looked up, you were almost off the road. That split second caused you to lose focus.

Don't lose your focus. That's when problems get worse and worse. Keep your eyes locked onto your Lord and Savior instead.

So now what? We've been trying to understand that our problems have purpose. We're at the end of this book and you're either both delivered and healed, or you're contending with the emotional decision of *what should I believe?*

Listen, You and God both can't be right! Although you may not understand how it works, don't do like most, reject anything you don't understand. You might be rejecting your opportunity to make a difference in a world that has been waiting on your birth for all eternity. You are not here by accident, and the mere fact that you're reading the close to this book suggests very strongly, you're searching for answers, your purpose, wondering where all of this is going to lead.

I can assure you when God created you in His image and His likeness, it was on purpose and with a purpose. He knew there would be people that wouldn't believe in Him, He knew there would be other belief systems to contend with Him, He knew people would turn to other gods, inciting His jealousy. He knew that some people would embrace the death of their Savior The Lord Jesus Christ, but wouldn't overcome the pressure of day-to-day living unless they saw someone else do it.

There's a person going through hell right now who needs somebody in Christ who had been through hell, possibly a few times, and only by the grace of God lived through it, not to be in bondage to it, but in spite of all the problems you've encountered in life, to become a witness and testify on the stand before judge and jury as:

- A _Character Witness,_ vouching for God's faithfulness and goodness

- An _Expert Witness,_ vouching for the validity of the process, no shortcuts, and the importance of trusting God through it.

- *And an <u>Eye Witness</u>,* ready to answer the question of the doubter, "how do you know it's going to work out?" and you can emphatically say, "I saw it with my own eyes!"

I like the way the Apostle Paul says it in *2 Corinthians 5:17-21:*

This means that anyone who belongs to Christ has become a new person. The old life is gone; a new life has begun!

And all of this is a Gift from God, who brought us back to himself through Christ. And God has given us this task of reconciling people to him. For God was in Christ, reconciling the world to himself, no longer counting people's sins against them. And he gave us this wonderful message of reconciliation. So we are Christ's Ambassadors; God is making his appeal through us. We speak for Christ when we plead, "Come back to God!" For God made Christ, who never sinned, to be the offering for our sin, so that we could be made right with God through Christ.

With every bad problem comes a great purpose…

God has given us the Greatest gift we could ever have, a Relationship with Him in the person of our Lord and Savior Jesus Christ.

It took Him accepting His problem, the brutality of the cross, in order to fulfill His purpose as the Lamb of God, The Savior of the world, our Redeemer, our Deliverer, our Healer, our Everything.

He taught us how to accept our problems in spite of how we feel about it, as directional signs from God, pointing us towards something that is directly tied to our existence for living - Our Purpose! Misunderstood by many, but divinely inspired by God, problems teach us how to completely depend upon God, trust in His Word, and live our lives to the Glory of God by Serving others.

Look at this in 2 Corinthians 5:18: *And all of this is a gift from God, who brought us back to himself through Christ (God's Purpose*). And God has given us this task (Our Purpose*) of reconciling people to him. *Emphasis Mine*

All your life, God has been using Problems to get you to embrace and walk out your multi-faceted Purpose.

What you thought was misfortune was divine intervention. Your life may have been a roller coaster but now you should know, God has had His hands on you the entire time.

Somebody is waiting for you to walk in your Purpose so they can be reconciled back to God - That is so Powerful, God is using your Purpose to help lead people out of hell and eternal separation from Him.

All of this to His Glory on Purpose...

Father I Thank You for my problems that have led me into a healthy relationship with you. I Thank You for problems though misunderstood in the beginning, taught me how to trust you through the process of restoration, deliverance and healing.

I Thank You that my purpose was in Christ's fulfillment of His purpose, and by accepting Him, I'm purposed to help reconcile others back to you with the

ministry of reconciliation and the message of reconciliation "Come Back To God!"

I Thank You that my Problems have Purpose in Jesus
name, Amen!

About The Author

A husband, father, pastor, entrepreneur, business professional and
life coach, Pastor Bozeman has been ministering for over 19 years
nationally and internationally, with a passionate style of direct,
expository, life-application preaching and teaching. From corporate
America to the inner city, Pastor Bozeman's commitment to serving
with excellence has influenced many to seek out the Lord Jesus
Christ and their God ordained purpose in life!

Pastor Bozeman now serves as the Sr. Pastor of New Beginnings Church of Atlanta, a church plant that launched its first worship service on 10-10-2010. NBCA is a "Christ Centered, Bible Based and Family Focused" ministry growing from the inside out. Pastor Bozeman also serves as the Director of Strategic Church Planting for the Intensify Fellowship of Churches headquartered in Chicago, IL and the Vice President of Operations for ProjectHood, a non-for profit organization serving impoverished communities in Chicago, IL under the direction of Pastor Corey B. Brooks.

Pastor Bozeman is a kingdom apostolic minister of deliverance and healing with an emphasis on spiritual warfare, prayer, and the training and development of gifts and callings. He is the host of "Relationships UnCut," a weekly biblical training conference call for singles and married couples interested in developing their relationships on all levels through pre-relationship coaching and post relationship counseling!

Pastor Bozeman studied at Oral Roberts University and is proficient in Systematic Theology, Apologetics, Urban Ministries, Pastoral Counseling, Church Systems and Operations and Leadership development. Pastor Bozeman is a spiritual father to many, residing in Atlanta, he has been happily married for 24 years and *counting* to Sheila, with 3 children, Steven Jr., Jade and Joshua.

Phone: 678-824-2968
Web: www.stevebozeman.com
Email: steve@stevebozeman.com
Facebook: Steve Bozeman
Twitter: PastorSBozeman

About SermonToBook.Com

SermonToBook.com began with a simple belief: that sermons should be touching lives, *not* collecting dust. That's why we turn sermons into high-quality books that are accessible to people all over the globe. Turning your sermon or sermon series into a book exposes more people to God's Word, better equips you for counseling, accelerates future sermon prep, adds credibility to your ministry, and even helps make ends meet during tight times.

John 21:25 tells us that the world itself couldn't contain the books that would be written about the work of Jesus Christ. Our mission is to try anyway. Because, in Heaven, there will no longer be a need for sermons or books. Our time is now.

If God so leads you, we'd love to work with you on your sermon or sermon series.

Visit www.sermontobook.com to learn more.

Made in the USA
San Bernardino, CA
09 August 2016